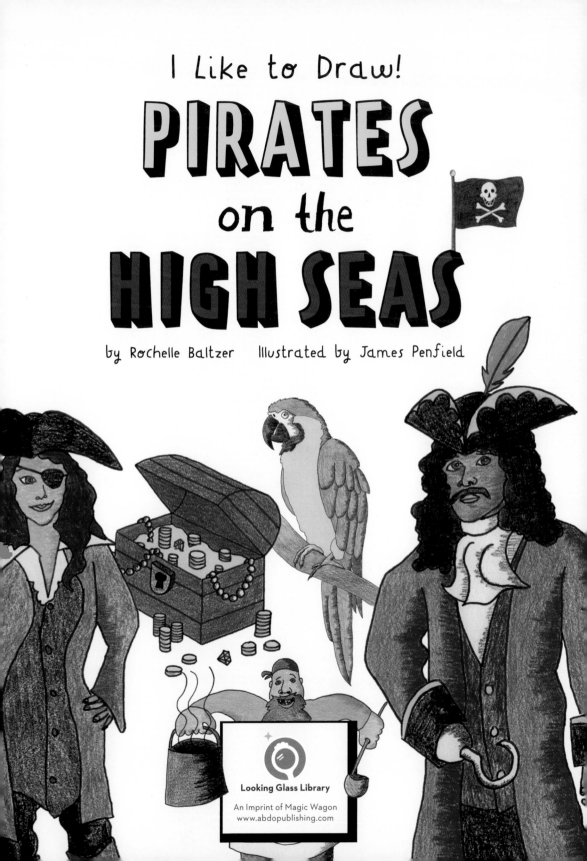

I Like to Draw!
PIRATES
on the
HIGH SEAS

by Rochelle Baltzer   Illustrated by James Penfield

Looking Glass Library
An Imprint of Magic Wagon
www.abdopublishing.com

www.abdopublishing.com

Published by Magic Wagon, a division of ABDO, PO Box 398166, Minneapolis, Minnesota 55439. Copyright © 2015 by Abdo Consulting Group, Inc. International copyrights reserved in all countries. No part of this book may be reproduced in any form without written permission from the publisher. Looking Glass Library™ is a trademark and logo of Magic Wagon.

Printed in the United States of America, North Mankato, Minnesota.
102014
012015

Cover and Interior Elements and Photos: iStockphoto, Thinkstock

Written by Rochelle Baltzer
Illustrations by James Penfield
Edited by Megan M. Gunderson, Bridget O'Brien
Cover and interior design by Candice Keimig

Library of Congress Cataloging-in-Publication Data

Baltzer, Rochelle, 1982- author.
  Pirates on the high seas / written by Rochelle Baltzer ; illustrated by James Penfield.
     pages cm. -- (I like to draw!)
  Includes index.
  ISBN 978-1-62402-084-1
  1. Pirates in art--Juvenile literature. 2. Drawing--Technique--Juvenile literature. I. Penfield, James, illustrator. II. Title.
  NC825.P57B35 2015
  741.2--dc23
                          2014037675

TABLE of CONTENTS

PIRATES on the HIGH SEAS

Ahoy, matey! So yeh like to draw pirates, do yeh? Welcome to the Golden Age of Piracy. The most famous swashbucklers sailed the high seas from the 1500s to the early 1800s. They plundered Spanish ships carrying treasure through the Caribbean. Let's step back in time and learn how to draw all things pirates!

STUFF YOU'LL NEED

Pencil

Paper

Eraser

Marker

Colored Pencils

KNOW THE BASICS

SHAPES

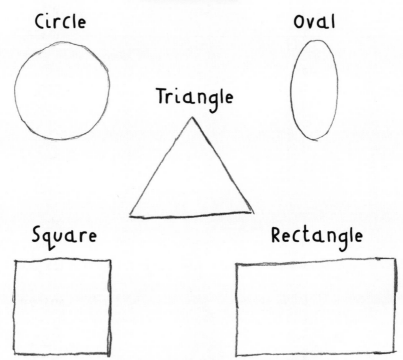

Circle

Oval

Triangle

Square

Rectangle

LINES
thick & thin

Straight

Wavy

Jagged

TALK LIKE AN ARTIST

Composition

Composition is the way parts of a drawing or picture are arranged. Balanced composition means having an even amount of parts, such as lines and shapes.

Unbalanced   Balanced

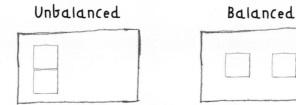

Dimension

Dimension is the amount of space an object takes up. Drawings are created on a flat surface and have length and width but not depth. So, they are two-dimensional. You can give an object depth by layering colors and adding shadow. This makes it look like it's popping off the page!

Without Dimension   With Dimension

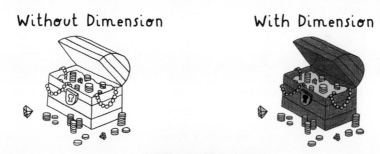

Shadow

Shadow is created by the way light shines on an object. Look outside on a sunny day. See how the sunlight shines on a tree? The side of the tree with more sunlight appears lighter than the other side.

Without Shadow   With Shadow

CAPTAIN

Sail ho, me hearties! The captain directed a pirate ship's crew. He took charge in times of battle. On many ships, the crew chose the captain for his leadership and naval skills. He did his best to guide the crew to treasure. He wanted to maintain his position and avoid a **mutiny**.

1 Draw an oval for the head, an oval for the body, and lines for the neck. Add a big pirate hat on top of the head.

2 Add a feather to the hat. Also add lines for arms and legs. Draw an oval for the hips.

3 Outline the body and add clothing. This captain has a long, open coat over a vest and dress shirt. Add eyes, a nose, a mouth, a mustache, and hair. And of course, add the famous hook to take the place of one hand!

4 Detail the clothing and finish outlining the body. Add fingernails.

ART TIP

Add simple, decorative lines to the hat to make your captain stand out. It's more important than just a plain old hat!

5 Outline the finished drawing with a thin, black marker.

6 Pirate captains loved lavish, richly colored clothing. Choose colors to make your captain look like a true scourge of the seven seas!

Kidd's Treasure

William Kidd was a famous Scottish pirate captain in the 1600s. Some people believe his treasure is still hidden somewhere.

9

QUARTERMASTER

The quartermaster was second in command on a pirate ship. This person was elected and had good management skills and sailing **expertise**. The quartermaster handled fights among crew members and decided what to do with prisoners.

1 Draw an oval for the head, an oval for the body, and lines for the neck. Add a floppy pirate's hat to the top of the head.

2 Draw lines for the arms and legs. Add an oval for the hips.

3 Outline the body and add clothing. Draw in the face and hair. Add an eye patch.

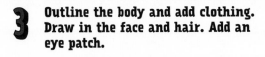

4 Detail the clothing. Add buttons to the vest and frills to the shirt.

5 Outline the finished drawing with a thin, black marker.

6 Color your quartermaster however you like! Using a traditionally feminine color can make your female pirate more identifiable as a female!

Ladies of the Sea
Women weren't usually allowed on pirate ships. So, some dressed as men to join a crew. Famous female pirates include Anne Bonny and Mary Read.

CARPENTER

Repairing a pirate ship was an important job. A ship's carpenter fixed deck boards, plugged holes, and mended sails. He regularly checked the ship's hull and masts to make sure they worked properly. Sometimes, a carpenter was taken prisoner from a looted ship and forced to work for a pirate crew.

 Draw an oval for the head and an oval for the body. Add a bandanna to the head and two lines connecting the head to the body.

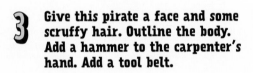

2 Draw lines for the arms, legs, and hips.

3 Give this pirate a face and some scruffy hair. Outline the body. Add a hammer to the carpenter's hand. Add a tool belt.

4 Draw tools on the tool belt. Add details to the pants and shirt. Finish the hands and boots.

ART TIP
Only add tools to the tool belt that you can fully recognize, not too many and not too little. Just draw enough so you can tell this is a tool belt!

5 Outline the finished drawing with a thin, black marker.

6 Color your carpenter. Use bright colors for the striped pants to make this pirate pop!

Doc on Board
If there was no doctor on a ship, the carpenter had to **amputate** people's limbs if they were badly hurt. He used a saw!

13

GUNNER

Fire in the hole! A ship's gunner gave a warning before he fired a cannon. He was in charge of loading and firing a pirate ship's cannons. He had to be careful because a cannon could blow up if handled wrong. It took great **accuracy** to hit a moving target!

1 Draw an oval for the head and an oval for the body. Draw lines for the neck. Add a bandanna to the head and hips to the bottom of the body.

2 Draw arms and legs. Outline the cannon and some cannonballs.

3 Draw a face and beard. Outline the body and draw clothing, including a belt. Outline a small pistol hanging from the belt. Add more detail to the cannon and a lit match in the gunner's hand so he can fire this cannon!

4 Detail the clothing and the rest of the body. Add highlights to the cannonballs, as they gleam in the sun.

ART TIP
A curved shape to the cannonballs makes them look three-dimensional, rather than flat circles.

5 Outline the finished drawing with a thin, black marker.

6 Have fun coloring your gunner! This guy can wear clothes of any color. Who knows where these swashbucklers pick up their clothing!

No Monkeying Around
A powder monkey cleaned the cannons and carried gunpowder to the gunner during battles. Powder monkeys were usually young boys.

COOK

A ship's cook had a tough job. There were not many ingredients to prepare meals for hungry pirates. When they could, cooks prepared fresh fish, turtle meat, and birds' eggs. But on long trips, staples were pickled meat and hardtack sea biscuits. Cooks were told to make food that tasted good, even if it was unhealthy.

1 Draw an oval for the head, a big circle for the body, and a small bandanna on top of the head.

2 Outline a big, bushy beard on the cook's face. Also outline an apron and lines for the arms and legs.

3 Outline the entire body, including the peg leg. Add a pot and a soup ladle to each one of his hands. Add eyes, a nose, and ears, and start the mouth.

4 Finish the mouth and add eyebrows. Draw buttons on the shirt and a pocket on the apron. Detail the peg leg, boot, hands, ladle, and pot.

ART TIP
When the eyebrow lines are drawn slanted down to the outside of the face, it gives your pirate a happy look!

5 Outline the finished drawing with a thin, black marker.

6 Color your cook. This pirate's apron is clean white, but you could color in some stains to make it look like he just cooked a big meal!

Dinner in the Dark
Sometimes, biscuits became infested with **weevils**. Still, pirates had to eat them. So, they went below deck so they couldn't see what they were eating!

SWAB

Aye, aye, cap'n! The swab, or swabbie, followed orders from the captain and the quartermaster. He scrubbed and mopped, or swabbed, the ship's deck. New or inexperienced pirates often started as swabs. Sometimes, pirates had to swab the deck if they got in trouble for bad behavior.

1 Draw an oval for the head and an oval for the body. Draw lines for the neck. Add a bandanna on the top of the head.

2 Outline a barrel and draw the swabbie sitting on it, holding a broom. Add lines for his arms, legs, and hips.

3 Draw a face and outline the rest of the body. Add detail to the barrel to give it dimension.

4 Finish the barrel and the mop. Detail the clothing, hands, and boots. Add long hair under the bandanna.

ART TIP

If you show a slight hint of the top dimension of the barrel, it will make the barrel and overall drawing look more realistic!

5 Outline the finished drawing with a thin, black marker.

6 Feel free to color the swabbie however you like!

Salt & Scum

Pirate ships could be at sea for months, so they were very dirty. Rats and insects lived on the ships. Cleaning ships was a job no one wanted.

PIRATE SHIP

Avast! Heave to! Pirate ships were different from today's boats. They didn't have engines, so the ships moved by the force of wind against large sails. Pirate ships were usually small but heavily armed. Swords, pistols, and cannons were on board, so crews were prepared to attack.

1 Outline the sails, the masts, and the ship itself.

2 Draw lines for the captain's quarters and circles for the cannon holes. Add the ram at the front of the ship.

3 Arch the sails so it looks like they're catching some wind! Detail the masts, and outline the pirate flag on top of the center mast. Add two lanterns to the back of the ship. Outline a sculpture of a brave seagoer on the front of the ship!

4 Add stripes to the sails. Draw a skull and crossbones on the pirate flag. Then, finish the sculpture of the brave seagoer leading the way!

ART TIP
Draw the pirate flag at an angle and with a wavy line, so that it looks like it's blowing in the wind!

5 Outline the finished drawing with a thin, black marker.

6 Color your pirate ship. Make the stripes on the sails whatever colors you like! Have fun designing your own, personal pirate ship!

Forceful Fleet
Sometimes, pirates kept the ships they looted. The stolen ships then became part of the captain's **fleet**.

PARROT

In drawings, a pirate is often shown with a parrot perched on his shoulder. Pirates took animals from islands they visited. Parrots, as well as small monkeys, were worth a lot of money because they were considered **exotic**. Wealthy people purchased parrots for their bright colors and ability to talk.

1 Draw a circle for the head, a shape for the beak, and an oval for the body.

2 Start the wings, tail feathers, and feet. Draw lines for a tree branch that this parrot is sitting on.

3 Outline the body and wings. Add jagged lines to the feathers for texture. Also draw the eye and beak, and define the feet a bit more.

4 Fully outline each feather on the wing and tail. Add a nostril to the face, and add claws to the feet.

ART TIP

Experiment with complementary colors. These look better to the eye. They include red and green, orange and blue, and purple and yellow!

5 Outline the finished drawing with a thin, black marker.

6 Parrots come in very bright colors. Have fun and color your parrot how you want!

Squddawk!
In the famous book Treasure Island by Robert Louis Stevenson, quartermaster Long John Silver has a pet parrot named Cap'n Flint.

JOLLY ROGER

A pirate crew created a flag to represent its ship. The most famous pirate flag is the Jolly Roger. It is black, with a white skull and crossbones. The term *Jolly Roger* was first used for the flag in 1700. This flag soon became a **symbol** of fear on the open seas.

1 Outline the flag, flagpole, and ball on top of the pole.

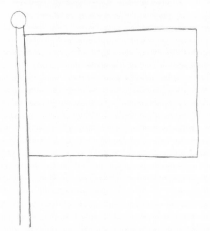

2 Add an oval for the skull. Draw lines beneath for the crossbones.

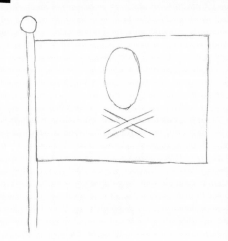

3 Draw ripples in the flag, so it looks like it's flapping in the wind! Outline the skull and crossbones.

4 Detail the skull and crossbones. Add a highlight to the ball on top of the flagpole.

ART TIP

To make it look like your skull only has a few teeth, draw all of the teeth first. Then, black out some of them!

5 Outline the finished drawing with a thin, black marker.

6 The famous Jolly Roger flag is black with white bones. Make the ball on top of the flagpole any color you like!

Warning Flag

During battle, pirates would raise a red flag to show they would give no quarter, or spare no lives.

TREASURE

To find the largest amount of treasure, or booty, was what every pirate yearned for. Booty was equally divided among crew members, with the captain getting twice the amount of a crew member. Scurvy dogs who stole more than their fair share were **marooned** on an island!

1 Outline the whole treasure chest.

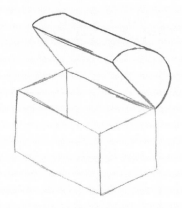

2 Think about where you want to draw stacks of coins, diamonds, and pearl necklaces. Then outline them inside and outside your ches Add a lock on the front.

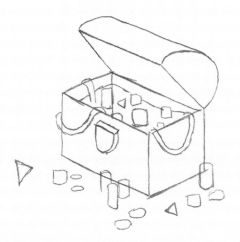

3 Fully detail the stacks of coins, diamonds, and necklaces.

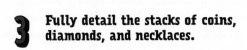
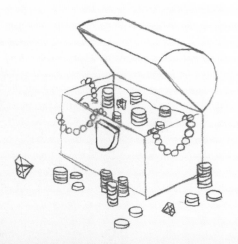

4 Draw lines for the wood boards that make up the structure of the chest. Also add a keyhole to the lock.

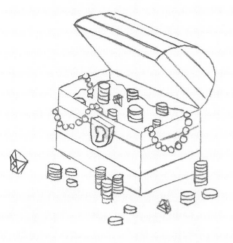

ART TIP

Diamonds can have a light blue color to them, but you can make them any gem you want just by changing the color!

5 Outline the finished drawing with a thin, black marker.

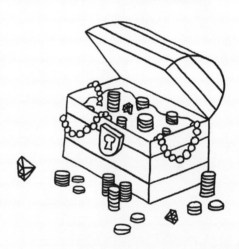

6 Color your treasure chest. Make your gold coins yellow or orange!

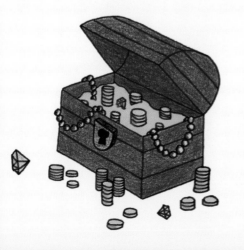

No Prey, No Pay
This was a common pirate law. It meant the crew was not paid, except by the loot they stole.

LOOK WHAT YOU CAN DRAW!

Treasure and Trivia

Pirates of the Caribbean Seas in the 1600s were called buccaneers.

Blackbeard was a British pirate known for being tough. He had a long, black beard that he braided and tied with ribbons. His real name was Edward Teach.

Besides striking ships, pirates attacked towns along coasts. They captured people as prisoners unless given money.

Many pirate ships attacked Spanish fleets traveling between Spain and its colonies in Mexico. They looted jewels, gold, and silver.

A pirate crew followed a code of conduct on the ship. Crew members took care of sick or wounded pirates. And, they worked together to share booty.

Many pirates were sea dogs, or experienced seamen, who could not find other work. Others became pirates in hopes of finding treasure and adventure.

Glossary

accuracy (A-kyuh-ruh-see) – the state of being free from mistakes.

amputate (AM-pyuh-tayt) – to cut off a body part.

exotic (ihg-ZAH-tihk) – interesting because it is strange or different from the usual.

expertise (ehk-spuhr-TEEZ) – special skill or knowledge.

fleet – a group of ships under one command.

maroon – to leave somewhere, such as on an island, without hope of escape.

mutiny – when a group of people refuse to obey a leader's orders, taking away that person's control.

symbol (SIHM-buhl) – an object or mark that stands for an idea.

weevil – a small bug that eats grains and seeds.

Websites

To learn more about I Like to Draw!, visit **booklinks.abdopublishing.com**. These links are routinely monitored and updated to provide the most current information available.

Index